Classic Tales

Level 2

CW00507065

The Ugly Duckling

Retold by Sue Arengo
Illustrated by Mirella Mariani

Contents

OXFORD

UNIVERSITY PRESS

 It is summer. A duck sits on her eggs. She sits and she waits. She waits and waits.

At last the eggs open.

'At last!' says the duck. 'My little ducklings!'

But one egg does not open.

'Mm,' says her friend. 'That egg is strange. Leave it.'

My little ducklings!

3

'Leave my egg?' says Mother Duck.
'No. I can't leave it.'

She sits down again and she waits.
At last the egg opens.

what an ugly duckling!

'Oh!' says Mother Duck to her friend.
'You're right. He is strange. What an ugly
duckling!'

Come on, ducklings!

But the ugly duckling can swim. He can swim very well. And Mother Duck is happy.

'Come on, ducklings!' she says. 'Let's go to the farm! I want all my friends to see you.'

'Hello, everyone,' she calls. 'Look at my little ducklings!'

'This is my family,' says Mother Duck.

'Very nice. Very nice,' say the ducks. 'But that duckling is very big. He's ugly!'

'He is strange,' they say. 'He's an ugly duckling.'

One of the ducks pecks him.

He is strange.

Go away, you ugly duckling!

Every day the farm girl comes.
Every day she kicks him.

'Go away, you ugly duckling!'
she says.

So one day the ugly duckling
runs away. He runs away from
the farm.

'Go! Yes, go!' say his brothers
and sisters. 'You're strange!
You're ugly!'

It's colder now. The ugly duckling
is bigger.

One day, two geese see him.

'Mm, you're strange!' they say.

'You're very ugly,' they say. 'But you're
interesting. Do you want to fly with us?'

Do you want to fly with us?

But suddenly there is a bang. Bang!
Bang! And the geese are dead.

There are some men. Men with guns
and dogs. The ugly duckling is afraid.

A big dog comes. He sees the ugly
duckling. And he looks at him. Then
the dog swims away.

'I am ugly,' says the ugly duckling.
'So he doesn't want to eat me.'

The ugly duckling runs away. He comes to an old hut and he goes in.

In the hut there is a woman, a cat, and a hen. The woman is old and she can't see.

'What's this?' she says. 'A duck? Ah! You can give me some eggs.'

You can give me some eggs.

'Come on,' says the cat. 'Where are your eggs?'

'I haven't got any,' says the ugly duckling.

'Then go!' says the hen.

The ugly duckling goes away. It is winter now. And it is very cold.

One evening the ugly duckling sees something wonderful and strange. Three swans! Three big, beautiful swans.

'Oh,' he cries. 'What beautiful birds! Big, beautiful, and free.'

He calls to them. 'Who are you? Take me with you.'

But they do not hear him.

Take me with you.

It is winter now. It is cold. There is ice on the water. So the ugly duckling can't swim.

A man sees him. He breaks the ice with his shoe.

'Poor bird!' he says. 'Come home with me.'

The man's children want to play.

'Come here!' they say.

But the ugly duckling runs away. He falls into the milk. The children laugh.

'Come here!' they say.

Then he falls into the butter. Oh dear! What a mess!

Come here!

Then he falls into the flour.

'Get out!' cries the man's wife.
'Get out of my house!'

The ugly duckling runs. Suddenly
he starts to fly.

The door is open. He flies up into
the sky.

Get out of my house!

He can fly! He can fly!

'I can fly!' says the ugly duckling.

And now the sun comes out. It is spring.
Then he sees a garden. A garden with
a river.

'What a beautiful garden!' he says.
And he flies down.

He sees something. He sees the swans. He sees the three swans.

'Oh! They are beautiful!' he says. 'I must speak to them.' But he is afraid.

He looks down at the water and he sees his face. He is not an ugly duckling any more. He is a beautiful swan too.

It's true. It's true! He's not a duckling. He's not a duck. He's a swan. He's a swan too.

Some children run down to the river.

'Look, Mother!' they say. 'A new swan! Look! Oh, look! Look at the new swan!'

'Yes,' she says. 'Isn't he beautiful!'

Exercises

1 What do they say? Write the words.

1 My _little ducklings!_

2 What an ugly _____ !

3 Where are your _____ ?

4 Take me _____ .

2 Where is the ugly duckling? Write the words.

1 in the ___egg___

2 in the _____

3 in the _____

4 in the _____

5 in the _____

6 in the _____

3 Make sentences about the story.
Then write them in the correct order.

He looks down in a river ...

A man takes him home ...

The ugly duckling runs ...

One day the ugly duckling runs away ...

He comes to an old woman's hut ...

The ducks say, ...

but the man's wife says, 'Get out!'

'That duckling is ugly!'

but the old woman's hen says, 'Go!'

and he sees a beautiful swan.

and suddenly he starts to fly.

from his brothers and sisters.

1 *The ducks say, 'That duckling is ugly!'*

2 _____

3 _____

4 _____

5 _____

6 _____

4 Put the words in the correct order.

1 me eggs You give can some.
   You can give me some eggs.

2 falls Then butter into the he.

   _____

3 more ugly any He not duckling an is.

   _____

4 ducks him One pecks the of.

   _____

Picture Dictionary

afraid *He's afraid.*

birds

cold *He's cold.*

dead *They're dead.*

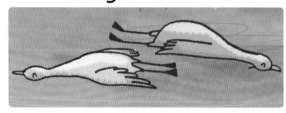

duck

duckling

face

farm

fly

garden

goose

geese

gun

river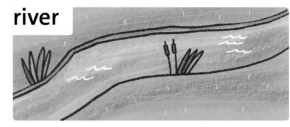

hen

spring *It's spring.*

ice

swan

kick

swim

laugh

ugly *He's ugly.*

peck

winter *It's winter.*

Classic Tales

Classic stories retold for learners of English – bringing the magic of traditional storytelling to the language classroom

For Classic Tales Teacher's Handbook, visit www.oup.com/elt/readers/classictales

Level 1: 100 headwords
- The Enormous Turnip
- The Lazy Grasshopper
- The Little Red Hen
- Lownu Mends the Sky
- The Magic Cooking Pot
- The Magpie and the Milk
- Mansour and the Donkey
- Peach Boy
- The Princess and the Pea
- Rumpelstiltskin
- The Shoemaker and the Elves
- Three Billy-Goats

Level 2: 150 headwords
- Amrita and the Trees
- Big Baby Finn
- The Fisherman and his Wife
- The Gingerbread Man
- Jack and the Beanstalk
- King Arthur and the Sword
- Rainforest Boy
- Thumbelina
- The Town Mouse and the Country Mouse
- The Ugly Duckling

Level 3: 200 headwords
- Aladdin
- Bambi and the Prince of the Forest
- Goldilocks and the Three Bears
- The Heron and the Hummingbird
- The Little Mermaid
- Little Red Riding Hood
- Rapunzel

Level 4: 300 headwords
- Cinderella
- Don Quixote: Adventures of a Spanish Knight
- The Goose Girl
- Sleeping Beauty
- The Twelve Dancing Princesses

Level 5: 400 headwords
- Beau and the Beast
- The Ma c Brocade
- Pinocchio
- Snow White and the Seven Dwarfs

OXFORD
UNIVERSITY PRESS

Great Clarendon Street, Oxford, OX2 6DP, United Kingdom

Oxford University Press is a department of the University of Oxford. It furthers the University's objective of excellence in research, scholarship, and education by publishing worldwide. Oxford is a registered trade mark of Oxford University Press in the UK and in certain other countries

© Oxford University Press 2011

The moral rights of the author have been asserted

First published in 2001

2020 2019 2018 2017 2016

20 19 18 17 16 15 14 13 12 11

ISBN: 978 0 19 423914 1   Book
ISBN: 978 0 19 424001 7   e-Book
ISBN: 978 0 19 423915 8   Activity Book and Play
ISBN: 978 0 19 401412 0   Audio Pack

Printed in China

This book is printed on paper from certified and well-managed sources

ACKNOWLEDGEMENTS

Illustrated by: Mirella Mariani/Plum Pudding Illustration